The Wec
Forecast

Written by Elspeth Graham
Illustrated by Mal Peet

Collins Educational
An imprint of HarperCollinsPublishers

It will be rainy.

It will be sunny.

It will be cloudy.

8

It will be windy.

It will be snowy.

It will be stormy.

There will be a rainbow.

rain

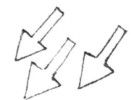

wind

sun

snow

cloud

storm